HOW TO BECOME A CONSULTANT TODAY

Mindset, Strategies, and Actions to Stand Out Locally and Internationally

Bertrand Ndeffo, Certified Leadership Coach, international speaker and consultant

With the collaboration of Eleonore Mejouong, international trainer, speaker and consultant

First edition

EducNation Consulting Inc.

Brampton, Ontario, Canada, March 2025

EducNation Consulting Inc.

HOW TO BECOME A CONSULTANT TODAY

Mindset, strategies and actions to stand out locally and internationally

Bertrand Ndeffo

Eleonore Mejouong

EducNation Consulting Inc.

17, Denlow Drive

Brampton, ON, L6Y 2L3

Canada

First edition, March 2025.

Published in Canada.

HOW TO BECOME A CONSULTANT TODAY

Mindset, Strategies, and Actions to Stand Out Locally and Internationally

Bertrand Ndeffo

Certified Leadership Coach, International Speaker, and Consultant

- Member of the Canadian Chamber of Commerce
- Member of the Certified Coaches Federation in Canada
- Member of the US Institute for Diplomacy and Human Rights
- Member of the Union des Commerçants de Côte d'Ivoire

In Collaboration with Eleonore Mejouong

International Trainer, Speaker, and Consultant

- Member of the Canadian Chamber of Commerce
- Member of the Union des Commerçants de Côte d'Ivoire

ABOUT THE AUTHORS

Bertrand Ndeffo

Bertrand Ndeffo is an international trainer, speaker, and consultant with over 20 years of corporate experience in Switzerland and Canada. His areas of expertise include education, communication, and international business.

In April 2016, Bertrand founded **EducNation Consulting Inc.** in Canada, a training and consulting firm offering coaching sessions, conferences, and both online and face-to-face training. Today, EducNation operates in approximately 20 countries.

Since January 2024, **EducNation Consulting Ivoire SARL** has been officially registered in Côte d'Ivoire (with CEPICI) and already collaborates with prominent partners such as:

- **Archipel Groupe Sarl**
- **Fontaine d'Or** (legal and accounting consultancy)
- **Agence Premium** (studies and travel in France)
- **Fondation Africa Light**
- **Collège Moderne de Togoniere**

From **July to November 2024**, EducNation Consulting Inc. provided staff training and communication services for **Archipel Groupe Sarl**, covering:

- Public speaking coaching
- Press relations
- Preparation of press briefings and conferences

- Managing the CEO's page and the company's LinkedIn page

Bertrand served as **Master of Ceremonies** and moderated a panel on investment opportunities in Côte d'Ivoire at the **sixth edition of the Salon International du Bâtiment et de la Construction (SIBAT, September 2024)** in Abidjan.

Bertrand and EducNation Consulting Inc. are members of:

- **Canadian Chamber of Commerce**
- **Certified Coaches Federation** (Canada)
- **US Institute for Diplomacy and Human Rights** (USA)
- **Ontario College of Teachers** (Canada)
- **Lean In organization** (founded by Sheryl Sandberg and Rachel Thomas)

EducNation Consulting Ivoire SARL is a member of the **Union des Commerçants de Côte d'Ivoire** and the **Haut Patronage des Commerçants et Opérateurs Économiques de Côte d'Ivoire**, with plans to join the **Ivory Coast Chamber of Commerce and Industry** in 2025.

Bertrand has built a vast professional and business network spanning 20 countries across four continents, including **Ivory Coast, Congo, DRC, Cameroon, Kenya, France, Switzerland, Canada, USA, Philippines,** and **China**.

Beyond his professional life, Bertrand has been an active parent, serving on his children's school councils for ten years — two as president — and as a board member of **Parents Partenaires en Éducation (PPE)**. In 2021, PPE awarded him the title of **"Engaged and Influential Parent"** and recognized his contribution to integrating immigrant families into Ontario's French-language schools. Bertrand also authored *Mise en contexte des conseils scolaires francophones ontariens: A Guide for Parents and Guardians.*

Eleonore Mejouong

Born in **Cameroon**, **Eleonore Mejouong** developed an early passion for learning and innovation. After completing her studies in Cameroon, she spent sixteen years in **Switzerland**, combining academic pursuits with professional experience, which greatly enriched her knowledge and skills.

Eleonore now resides in **Canada** with her children, working in the vital field of **cybersecurity** at a well-known institution.

As an accomplished entrepreneur, Eleonore co-owns two brands:

- **B&E** — a shea butter brand
- **B.en.Or** — a lingerie brand (www.benorharmony.com)

Her entrepreneurial spirit is matched by her dedication to inspiring positive change and transforming mindsets. She is deeply curious about people and cultures, which fuels her passion for travel. Recent trips to **China, Kenya,** and **Ivory Coast** have strengthened her appreciation for cultural diversity and local traditions.

Ever eager to learn and open to new perspectives, Eleonore Mejouong continues to be a dynamic and inspirational figure, both in her professional work and personal endeavors.

March 10 2020

To Whom It May Concern:

This is to confirm that EducNation Consulting Inc., member number 049054, is a member in good standing with the Canadian Chamber of Commerce.

We attest to the company's expertise and support the steps taken by its representatives.

Respectfully,

Jean Jacques Hermans
Senior Vice-President, Corporate relations
Canadian Chamber of Commerce | Chambre de commerce du Canada
590 – 999 Boul. De Maisonneuve | Montréal, QC H3A 3L4

RECOMMENDATIONS

Bertrand is passionate about education. He is determined to educate and empower all those in need.

His listening skills are impressive.

His spirit of collaboration is second to none.

A remarkable, unrivalled leader.

An accomplished, competent and well-informed professional. I recommend him without hesitation.

Bertrand is passionate about education. He is determined to educate and equip all those in need to take better care of themselves. His listening skills are impressive. His spirit of collaboration is second to none. A remarkable, unparalleled leader. A consummate professional, competent and well-informed. I recommend him without hesitation.

Sylvie Dan, TOGAF, PMP, CCBA, ITIL, CSM

Founder and CEO, Ovation Consult, award-winning artificial intelligence company (USA)

I've known Bertrand for several years and have always appreciated his expertise and the seriousness of his approach. I sincerely recommend him. His international relations and project management skills are second to none.

Jean-Jacques Hermans, General Manager, La Guilde du jeu vidéo du Québec

Bertrand is a seasoned education consultant and inspirational communicator.

I had the pleasure of taking part in conferences given by Bertrand, notably on leadership and educational development in Africa. His international experience (Canada, Switzerland, France, Cameroon, Congo), cultural sensitivity and active listening skills have left a lasting impression on me.

Today, in Canada and elsewhere, many organizations are snapping up Bertrand's expertise. You'd do well to emulate them.

Frederic William Kingue, Employment and Personal Branding Coach, 3 X LinkedIn Top Choice Africa (Ivory Coast)

It is an absolute privilege to write this recommendation for my esteemed colleague, Bertrand Ndeffo. Bertrand is an outstanding leader and consultant in the fields of education, international trade, talent management and business analysis. Having had the opportunity to work with Bertrand through Helping Hands as part of Ovation Consult, I experienced first-hand his deep expertise, unwavering commitment and visionary approach to mentoring and consulting.

Bertrand has an extraordinary ability to navigate the complexities of education and international business, while fostering an environment where talent and potential can flourish. His knowledge of business analysis is second to none, always grounded in strategic thinking and forward-looking perspectives. In our mentoring collaborations, Bertrand's ability to guide both mentees and mentors with clarity, wisdom and empathy has been a true inspiration.

As a mentor, Bertrand consistently demonstrates his passion for empowering others. His approach is holistic - he not only shares his vast knowledge and experience, but also invests time in understanding the individual needs and goals of those he works with. He has an incredible talent for identifying strengths and providing the tools and encouragement needed to maximize potential. His mentoring has helped us develop both professionally and personally, and I've seen the same impact on mentees in our community.

Bertrand's leadership of Helping Hands as part of Ovation Consult has created a thriving community of mentors and mentees where knowledge, experience and support are freely shared. His ability to foster collaboration and continuous learning has made a significant difference to the lives of all those fortunate enough to work with him. His dedication to mentoring is not just professional, it's deeply personal and shines through in every interaction.

Bertrand, I am deeply grateful for our collaboration and for your advice. Your expertise, combined with your generosity of spirit, has had a profound impact. I look forward to continuing to learn from you and to the many future collaborations that will undoubtedly advance our shared vision of empowering others. Thank you for being an extraordinary mentor and colleague!

Mark Burnett, Project Manager, Founder and Author, *The Ambidextrous Project Manager* (Jamaica)

I had the privilege of benefiting from exceptional, special and enriching coaching with Mr Bertrand. His teaching skills and background enabled me to improve certain aspects of my professional life, but also to develop and better manage my personal assets. From coaching on how to maintain our image through social networks to skills development, I was amazed by both his theoretical and practical knowledge of the professional sector. It was a great pleasure for me to work alongside him for a long time, but above all to benefit from his training.

What's more, his expertise in public speaking and management of corporate networks make him the perfect person to work with. I highly recommend him for your corporate and personal training needs.

Lucien Zahibo, Legal and Projects Manager, Union des Commerçants de Côte d'Ivoire

We were lucky enough to welcome Mr. Ndeffo to our Associate Teacher Additional Qualification course. In front of over 50 teachers, he presented his immigrant and professional career path, from university studies in education, his internship experiences, then as an associate teacher, to his current role as a coach and mentor. Mr. Ndeffo gave an eloquent presentation, highlighting with concrete examples from his own experience the elements that make the difference in supporting interns, as well as avenues of professional development for welcoming interns and guiding them in our role as teachers in Ontario. We look forward to working with Mr. Ndeffo again, and wish him every success in his promising projects.

Fatima Khlifi, educational consultant (Canada)

I met Bertrand at a seminar on education in Pointe-Noire/Congo-Brazzaville. I was immediately seduced by his empathy, his ability to listen, his ease of communication, his ability to make himself understood by anyone, his open-mindedness and his simplicity. Leader and founder of EducNation Consulting Inc, Bertrand is passionate about education and approachable. The future of young people is at the heart of his concerns. Very available to others, Bertrand and I spent some excellent time sharing experiences at our firm. He is a brilliant international speaker. As a passionate trainer myself, I've learned a lot about learning methods from Bertrand!

Zephirin Kimbouri-Ntsatou, international consultant, certified tax advisor CEMAC no. CF 345 (Congo)

Bertrand is an outstanding host who is not afraid to take on new challenges. He has a wonderful charisma, and his desire to help others is greatly appreciated by all.

Nathalie Lachance, Communications Coordinator, Parents Partenaires en Éducation (Canada)

It's rare in our French-speaking microcosm to meet people who make themselves available to listen to you, to reach out to you, and to share a moment of humanity. Such encounters have even greater impact when these people share their knowledge and skills, with great generosity and always with humility. I see Bertrand Ndeffo as a leader who understands the meaning of the word, not as someone who takes pleasure in shining at the top all by himself, but as someone who strives to stimulate the potential of others, with a view to inspiring other leaders.

Elykiah (Odette) E. Doumbe, Founder, UPn'DO (Canada)

As a student in your French course, I experienced first-hand your unwavering dedication to promoting a positive and inclusive learning environment. Your passion for the subject was evident in every class and activity, which piqued my curiosity and enthusiasm for literature. Your ability to explain complex concepts with clarity and patience enabled me to grasp and apply knowledge effectively.

Outside the classroom, you always went above and beyond your teaching responsibilities. Your door was always open for students who needed extra help or advice. Your accessibility and willingness to provide individualized attention really made a difference in my educational journey. Your genuine interest in your students' success didn't stop with their studies, as you also offered valuable advice and support on a personal level. Your mentoring played an important role in shaping my character and aspirations.

In addition, your exceptional organizational skills ensured that each course was well structured and engaging. Your use of a variety of teaching methods, including visual aids, group activities and real-life examples, facilitated a dynamic and interactive learning experience. You encouraged open discussion and fostered an atmosphere of respect and intellectual curiosity. These qualities not only facilitated my personal growth, but also cultivated a strong sense of community among my peers.

I'm particularly grateful for the opportunities you've given us outside the school program. Whether organizing excursions, coordinating extracurricular activities or encouraging participation in academic competitions, you have always sought to enhance our educational experience. These experiences enabled me to apply the knowledge I gained in the classroom to real-world scenarios and develop essential skills such as teamwork, critical thinking and problem-solving.

Your commitment to ongoing professional development was evident in the innovative teaching methods you implemented. You frequently attended workshops and seminars to keep abreast of the latest advances in education, and your willingness to adapt and incorporate new techniques into the classroom inspired my passion for lifelong learning.

It was an honor to be one of your students.

Carlo Duchemin, Marine Operations Coordinator (France)

Bertrand is a committed, patient and inquisitive professional. I have benefited enormously from our various exchanges on education, transmission and values.

Congratulations Bertrand for all you do!

Adamou Boubacar, Director, Sahel Agropole, Professor of Biotechnology, President of the Sahel Institute for Global Defense and Security (Niger and France)

Bertrand is passionate about education and personal development. I couldn't recommend him more highly for his talents.

William Talehc, Director, Salon International de l'Entreprise PROMOTE (Cameroon)

Members of the Ladies in suits, Lean In circle were delighted to welcome Bertrand Ndeffo as a special guest for the November 2021 workshop. He was an incredible guest, with solid experience in the fields of education, communication and leadership.

The theme of this workshop was "How words affect our thoughts, our subconscious and our actions". Bertrand shared with us key tools for strategic thinking and influential communication. He emphasized the impact of a daily positive inner dialogue to push our minds to excel and realize our professional and personal aspirations.

He also used different formats for his presentation (presentation techniques, audios, videos and poetry). The whole presentation immersed us, encouraged us to stay focused and understand the importance of keeping a positive mindset.

A 100% repeat experience! Thanks Bertrand!

Ghislaine Y. Aniambossou, Communications Manager (England, France)

I highly recommend Bertrand Ndeffo, an exceptional coach whom I've known for almost two years. His leadership, empathetic listening and caring guidance are remarkable. Always positive and passionate, Bertrand inspires and guides others with genuine expertise and humanity.

Adèle Gunn, educational consultant (Canada)

I had the privilege of working with Bertrand Ndeffo for a few months and was constantly impressed by his skills and qualities.

Bertrand is a natural leader who inspires and motivates those around him. He has a clear vision and knows how to turn it into reality. He is also an excellent communicator and knows how to address different audiences.

In addition to being an exceptional leader, Bertrand is also an outstanding coach. He has an innate ability to identify people's strengths and weaknesses and help them develop to their full potential. He is patient, encouraging and always ready to lend a hand.

Bertrand is also a very empathetic and caring person. He really cares about the people around him and is always there to support them. He knows how to create a positive and friendly atmosphere.

A concrete example of Bertrand's impact on my life is his invaluable help with my immigration process to Canada. I was initially intimidated by the complexity of the process and lacked self-confidence. Bertrand gave me hope by providing encouragement and sound advice. Thanks to his exceptional coaching, I was able to overcome my fears and achieve my goal of immigrating to Canada.

An anecdote that illustrates Bertrand's personality is the time he encouraged me to make a video. I'm very shy by nature and don't like to show myself in public. Bertrand believed in me and encouraged me to get out of my comfort zone. Thanks to his encouragement and support, I was able to make the video and I'm very proud of it today.

Bertrand Ndeffo is a rare and precious person. He is an exceptional leader, an outstanding coach and a wonderful friend.

Chimène Mamno, teacher and entrepreneur (Cameroon, Canada)

Demanding of himself, Bertrand is a man of unparalleled professionalism. I've known him for eight years. We've worked together as PISA assessors, teachers (at different levels) and, above all, as literary critics for POUR PARLE PROFESSION, the magazine of the Ontario College of Teachers.

His mastery of the written word and his deep involvement in the field of education shine through every day in his written and media contributions.

He is capable of leading, advising and driving the education debate forward with a realistic and optimistic vision.

On a personal level, Bertrand is a person of integrity, benevolent, generous with his expertise, and whose sense of analysis and observation sometimes surprises and always enriches.

I highly recommend Bertrand as a useful educational tool.

Lucienne Béatrice Koua Dubé, Special Education Consultant (Canada)

DEDICATION

To my parents.

Eternal gratitude.

Bertrand

To my mother Florence.

Thank you for being you.

Eleonore

EPIGRAPH

When we give with joy and accept with gratitude, everyone is blessed.

Maya

Service to others is the rent you pay for your room here on earth.

Mohammed Ali

TABLE OF CONTENTS

WARNING

This book is designed to provide information on how to become a consultant, promote your services and position yourself as a leader.

If you need legal assistance or other expertise, you should seek the services of a competent professional.

This book is not intended to provide all the information available to the authors and/or publisher, but rather to complement and amplify other texts.

We strongly advise you to read the documentation available online or elsewhere on the subject, to learn as much as you can about the consulting profession, and to adapt this information to your individual needs.

Consulting is not a get-rich-quick scheme.

Anyone who decides to become a consultant can expect to devote a great deal of time and effort.

DISCLAIMER OF LIABILITY

Every effort has been made to make this book as complete and accurate as possible; however, errors, both typographical and of content, may occur. Consequently, this text should only be used as a general guide, and not as the ultimate source of information on how to become a consultant and grow your business.

In addition, this book contains information on the consulting field which may no longer be valid at the time of reading.

The aim of this book is to educate and entertain.

The authors shall not be liable to any person or entity for any loss or damage caused, or claimed to be caused, directly or indirectly, by the use of this book or by the information contained in this book.

If you do not wish to be bound by the above, you may return this book to the publisher for a full refund.

THE JOY OF BEING A CONSULTANT

B ecoming a consultant means saying no to routine. Becoming a consultant means enjoying Mondays as much as Fridays. Becoming a consultant means offering your expertise locally as well as internationally. Becoming a consultant means moving from hourly wages to potentially unlimited income.

Becoming a consultant means refusing to exhaust yourself in the metro-work-dodo race. Becoming a consultant means choosing the freedom to choose your projects and contracts.

Becoming a consultant means multiplying your impact today and your contribution to the well-being of future generations.

THE STATE OF CONSULTATION WORLDWIDE

The consulting sector has experienced significant growth worldwide in recent years, driven by changing business needs, technological advances and a growing demand for specialized expertise in a variety of sectors.

For example, the global management consulting market was valued at around US$300 billion in 2023, and projections indicate that it could reach over US$400 billion by 2028.

This growth was particularly marked in the IT consulting and technology services sectors, because the demands of digital transformation and cybersecurity were especially strong.

Here are a few important points to consider.

- Digital transformation: as companies embrace new technologies such as AI, blockchain and cloud computing, demand is growing for consultants who can help them strategize, implement and optimize these technologies.

- Sustainability and ESG: environmental, social and governance (ESG) initiatives have spurred growth in consulting, as organizations seek advice on integrating sustainable practices.

- Post-pandemic recovery: the need for strategic guidance in the post-COVID-19 era has fueled demand in a variety of sectors, including healthcare, finance and supply chain.

- North America and Western Europe remain the largest markets for consulting services. However, the Asia-Pacific region, in particular countries such as China and India, is set to experience stronger growth over the coming years.

- In emerging markets such as West Africa, there is a growing demand for local consulting firms, particularly in areas such as infrastructure, regulatory compliance and digital business models. We have seen this on successive visits to Côte d'Ivoire, where consulting needs are not just limited to the above areas, but also touch on real estate and agribusiness, among others.

- Management and strategy consulting still accounts for a significant share of the market, but IT and technology consulting has seen the fastest growth, thanks to companies like Accenture, Deloitte and PwC expanding their technology and cybersecurity practices.

- More and more customers are looking for specialist consultants in areas such as data science, cybersecurity and AI strategy, hence the rise of specialist, independent consultancies.

- In the healthcare consulting sector, the pandemic has accelerated the need for digital healthcare solutions, and companies are increasingly seeking advice on how to improve patient care through technology.

- Financial services and regulatory compliance are growth areas for consultants, especially as global markets face increased scrutiny and regulatory complexity.

Whether on a small or large scale, according to our research and observations in North America, Europe, Asia and Africa, no industry is immune to the demand for consultants, especially as remote working and hybrid models have become increasingly common, enabling companies to tap into a global talent pool.

The meteoric rise of AI worldwide will lead consultants to focus more on high-level consulting services, while routine, low-value tasks can be handled by automated systems.

Consulting projections for the next 10 years point to a growing demand for strategic advice in an increasingly complex global environment.

It's the perfect time to get trained and enter the consulting arena!

WHAT ARE YOU WAITING FOR TO BECOME A CONSULTANT?

D on't wait until you have all the answers to go on a trip. Go on a journey to find all the answers.

Soon, EducNation Consulting Inc. will be 9 years old! Nine years of impact in Canada and in at least 20 countries on four continents!

This morning, I had the privilege of sharing my expertise in education and human rights with the friendly staff of the Conseil scolaire du Grand Nord (Ontario).

A few weeks ago, I spoke in France, Cameroon and Ivory Coast.

Soon...

Wherever I go, whether face-to-face or online, it's the same fervor and satisfaction: the kind that comes from extraordinary encounters, fascinating conversations and surprising discoveries.

The first and most important of these? Discovering yourself, your potential, your aspirations and your passions.

Becoming a consultant means saying no to self-sufficiency. Becoming a consultant means having the courage to push your limits. To become a consultant is to take your fellow human beings by the hand and walk with them.

What are you waiting for to become a consultant?

An infinite world of possibilities opens up to you. All you have to do is open your arms to it.

A STATE OF MIND

In January 2025, I posted in a Facebook group the text entitled "My most formidable weapon as a consultant" (available in this book), accompanied by a photo of myself alongside a member of a flight attendant.

As much as this publication has received praise (15 people have liked it), it has also generated criticism, which I'll dwell on for a moment here.

But first, here they are:

"I remember that everyone is a consultant in Canada."

"So you made a description with a woman who forces a smile as we can notice with the concentration of her eyes and the tense face... and that makes a consultant, maybe in Canadian depression yes!"

"Did you go through the control room?"

"I'm just curious: for you, being a consultant means filming yourself with everyone who passes by?

Because we wanted to read what you have to say on your area of expertise and not your photos unless you're a publicist..."

Do you want to know how I reacted to this emotional outburst? I thanked everyone for their contribution. The last thing you want to do is explain or justify yourself to anyone, least of all to an unrestrained horde.

Many people live in 2025 with images in their heads from 10 or more years ago. Wouldn't a consultant who takes photos be one? Do you have to have white hair or 50 years of professional experience to call yourself a consultant? Would a consultant be recognizable by his or her face?

No, these people are not to blame. Google the word "consultant". What do you see? A consultant is said to have at least a master's degree. You are told the daily fee for a consultant.

Seriously!

A consultant can work successfully without a university degree. An intelligent or well-trained consultant knows that his or her fees depend on the complexity of the problem to be solved, its urgency and the organization that has called upon his or her expertise. The time taken to find the solution determines little or nothing about the value of the service. The consultants Eleonore and I have trained know the importance of using social networks to extend their visibility and reinforce their credibility. They have long understood that being a consultant is not a job, but a way of life. As much as I take photos and videos of the conferences and training courses I offer, I also take photos on flights, in airports, in waterfront restaurants in Bassam. In fact, I document my life as a consultant, which includes professional activities and meetings as much as moments of relaxation.

What's more, today's avangardist consultants accept mandates and then delegate a greater or lesser part of their tasks. How, you ask? If you're like me, you don't like repetitive tasks, or you don't try to do everything yourself in order to diversify your projects, explore new avenues of collaboration or enjoy life. At www.fiverr.com, you'll find professionals who can provide you with a multitude of services at reasonable cost.

Finally, why not take advantage of artificial intelligence? Here are a few platforms that will transform your daily life as a consultant in terms of time savings and productivity.

- **ChatGPT** for answers to almost any question.
- **Perplexity AI** for searching.
- **Github Copilot** lets you code.
- **Notion AI** useful for note-taking.
- **Midjourney** generates images.
- **Adobe Firefly** lets you edit images.
- **Claude** simplifies the writing.
- **ElevenLabs** gives us another voice.
- **Quillbot** improves your grammar.
- **CanvaMagic** helps you create resources.
- **Gemini** answers questions instantly.
- **Zapier** relieves you of repetitive tasks.
- **Adobe Acrobat** summarizes PDF documents.
- **Jasper** assists with content creation.
- **Runway** modifies videos.
- **Fireflies** provides the transcription.
- **Clockwise** schedules meetings.

THE KEY LIES IN YOUR THOUGHTS

A t a time when many people are wishing each other health and prosperity, if there's one wish I'd like to make for all of us on a daily basis, it's that we learn to renew our thoughts.

A strange vow? Of course not! Everything begins and ends with a thought. Thoughts precede our actions and decisions. The quality of our thoughts influences our health, our well-being, our relationships, our social interactions, our future, our life. The world is governed by thoughts. Around us, on the roads, in airport terminals, in factories, in homes, everywhere, we see thoughts talking, moving, acting.

For better or worse.

It's distressing to see the gap between the importance of thoughts in our lives and the time we devote to them. How many minutes a day do you devote to becoming aware of the thoughts that arise and grow within you and with you? Do you write them down? Do you ask yourself where they come from, what they mean and what you should do with them? Are they thoughts that galvanize you, uplift you and others? Or the other way round?

Several times a day, we perform our personal and dental hygiene. Several times a year, we change the oil in our cars. How many times a week, a month, a year do we clean our minds?

Unfortunately, hygiene and thought engineering aren't taught in schools, and they don't often feature in family conversations. So it's up to each and every one of us to do the work on ourselves, preferably with the help of a professional.

The key to our health, well-being and prosperity lies in the quality and development of our thoughts. Let's stop running and learn to think better.

WHAT ARE YOU AFRAID OF?

———◇———

Contrary to what many people think, there's no such thing as job security.

One day, you learn through the media that your employer has gone bankrupt and that your pension fund is likely to suffer.

For your neighbor, it's a question of "restructuring" the company while she's on maternity leave. The result? Her position has suffered, and she's having to relearn how to write a CV.

As for your brother-in-law, his outspokenness led to the non-renewal of his employment contract.

And then, one day while grocery shopping, you meet the mother of your son's best friend, who tells you that a fire has just reduced the factory where she's worked for 30 years to ashes.

In fact, job security becomes a reality the day you realize that it doesn't exist.

I beg your pardon?

Yes, it only exists when you realize it doesn't exist!

So, from that day on:

You stop worrying about losing your job;

You are constantly training to improve your skills;

Develop your professional network locally and internationally;

You're looking for one or more mentors;

You develop your personal brand;

You put your expertise and experience to work for the greatest number of people;

You forge strategic partnerships and collaborations;

And you enjoy both your newfound freedom and your impact on the lives of your fellow human beings.

You see, there's nothing to be afraid of!

CLIMB ONTO THE BALCONY

---◇---

S everal years ago, I took a course on leadership in education (I've taken others since, in education and other fields) during which the instructor often repeated to us, "Get on the balcony."

In fact, we had to analyze case studies, refer to the laws and regulations governing education in Ontario, and make decisions as leaders of an educational organization or community.

In the early days, our approach lacked perspective, and was too focused on the detail of individual actions rather than on the objectives of the management team, the spirit of the laws and regulations, and the well-being and future of the community.

The trainer therefore taught us to "climb onto the balcony", i.e. to look at the details without losing sight of the panorama, to take account of individuals without sacrificing the group, to read the present with the glasses of the future.

In today's uncertain and sometimes chaotic world, the ability to stand on the balcony and analyze any situation is an essential skill. It is the hallmark of leaders - people who can control their emotions in troubled times, look beyond their current circumstances and stay focused on personal development and mission accomplishment.

A POWERFUL
TECHNIQUE

S ome people may find it difficult to climb onto the balcony in certain situations. A powerful technique would be to physically move to a higher location. In other words, literally, get on the balcony.

For example, a mountain (or the top of a hill) or a café on the third floor of a building could serve as a balcony. There's a correlation between our actions, our emotions and our mental dispositions. Here, patiently, reconsider the problem you're facing from the point of view of everyone involved. Think about the consequences of your eventual decision and ask yourself what the consequences would be in at least five years' time. Take notes and re-read them two or three days later, before making your final decision.

This powerful technique will have enabled you to create a distance between the events and yourself, to let the dust settle and gain clarity, and to grasp certain nuances that were invisible at the outset.

FIVE STRATEGIES FOR A WINNING WEEK

B ecause the first musical notes determine the rest of the song, it's important to start the week with clarity and determination.

Here are five strategies to help you do just that.

1. Cultivate gratitude

Whatever your current situation, appreciate the fact that you're alive and able to read this text. In a notebook or file, every morning when you wake up, write down five things you're grateful for.

2. Determine your day's main objective

Do this for each day. What do you want to accomplish today? The day's goal should fit into the week's goal, and the week's goal into the month's goal.

3. Control your fears and doubts

It's normal to doubt yourself and your ability to achieve. That's why it's so important to keep your eyes on your goals. The encouragement and sound advice of a mentor or coach will help you keep both hands on the wheel of your future, and see what is still waiting to manifest itself before your very eyes.

4. Take action

Do what you can, with what you have, where you are. Every day, every week, take a step towards your goals. Celebrate each step for what it is: a victory over your inner and outer obstacles.

5. Enjoy the little things in your daily life

Life is full of little pleasures that we no longer see because we take them for granted. We need to start noticing and appreciating them again.

You'll have a week full of action and meaning!

THE THREE
KNOWLEDGES

In high school or university, you were undoubtedly told that there are three types of knowledge: knowing, knowing how to be and knowing how to do (and even a fourth: knowing how to do). These three types of knowledge enable you to find a job, build a career and find your place in society.

Today, let's classify knowledge differently. This is part of a logic of self-discipline, open-mindedness and ongoing personal and professional growth.

Here are three types of knowledge: what I know, what I don't know and what I don't know that I don't know.

WHAT I KNOW

We often know what we know. If we sometimes doubt our abilities or skills, it's because we lack self-confidence, or because we live in a harmful social environment.

Sometimes, too, we think we know something when we don't. So let's be humble. So let's be humble and ask questions of those more experienced than ourselves, or do a little more research to learn more about the subject.

Solution

Keep a portfolio of our achievements. Keep recognition cards and e-mails from colleagues, customers, business partners and family members. Let's display some of these trophies in our workspaces, at work and at home, and reread them from time to time.

WHAT I DON'T KNOW

In an increasingly specialized world, what we know or think we know is just a drop in the ocean of knowledge. What we don't know therefore forces us to be humble, and helps develop our curiosity.

Solution

Let's become students of our lives as well as of life. Let's take advantage of the training offered by our employers, even if it doesn't excite us that much. Finally, let's share our expertise with others to strengthen them and learn from them.

WHAT I DON'T KNOW THAT I DON'T KNOW

This form of knowledge is the most difficult to develop, because it requires a very high level of awareness, extraordinary curiosity and a strong desire to work on oneself and bring value to others.

Solution

Let's consider every moment and every event in our lives as a source of learning.

For example, a masterclass by industrialist Bertin Tchoffo at the "Back to Africa" Forum organized in Paris by Philippe Simo, a conversation with table neighbors at Dabali Xpress in Abidjan, reading books such as OPTION B by Sheryl Sandberg and Adam Grant and EMOTIONAL INTELLIGENCE by Daniel Goleman, or a solitary walk along Lake Geneva on a May morning.

It's by cultivating these three skills that you become a person of great worth, every day a little more.

THREE STRATEGIES TO REACH THE TOP

W hile I was giving an online training course a few days ago on the importance of developing your professional network and how to achieve it, one participant commented, "We have a lot of potential and great CVs, but it's the opportunities and recommendations that are lacking."

In fact, this young professional put his finger not on the problem, but on the consequences engendered by the problem.

There are three major mistakes that most people make on their career path.

1. Not having a coach

No one can imagine a tennis player winning a major tournament without a coach, can they? And yet so many employees say they don't need a coach. Others feel that paying a coaching professional is like throwing money out the window. Some, in some countries, even compare coaches to charlatans.

Each person has their own opinions and each person has their own results.

I'd advise you to choose your coach based on these three criteria:

1. Academic background and certifications. Is this person qualified to accompany you?

2. Membership of a professional organization. Your coach's work will be guided by standards and work ethics. You'll know where to file a complaint if need be.

3. Its impact or results. Ask your potential coach to show you testimonials from people he or she has coached. Research this professional online to gauge his or her reputation.

2 . Not having a mentor

If the coach helps you optimize your processes, improve your well-being and increase your productivity, the mentor prevents you from making the same mistakes, serves as a reference and opens the door to his or her business or professional network.

3. Not belonging to a group

We're all familiar with the adage that those who want to go fast go it alone, and those who want to go far go in a group. Personally, I find that joining a group of professionals looking in the same direction enables its members to go both far and fast. How do you do this? You benefit from the power of the collective brain and as many networks as there are members in the group.

In the end, hiring a coach, finding a mentor and taking part in masterminds can save you a lot of time in achieving your business or professional goals. At the same time, our quality of life and social impact increase tenfold.

SPEAK IN PUBLIC AND CHANGE YOUR LIFE

For many people, public speaking is a source of stress, fear and even panic. We don't like it, we don't want to make any mistakes, we avoid the judgment of others. What if we look ridiculous? What if we don't live up to expectations? What if we make mistakes? What if we... What if we...

You understand, speaking in front of an audience is first and foremost a question of self-confidence, a matter of feeling competent. Language quality, eloquence and oratory techniques come a long way behind.

The good news is that everyone, yes everyone, can develop the confidence to speak in front of an audience, large or small, on or off camera, with confidence, calm, self-assurance, simplicity and effectiveness.

Whatever your personality type, introvert or extrovert, you can learn to communicate your ideas, motivate your colleagues or convince potential business partners.

If I can do it, so can you. Before I became the international consultant and lecturer I have been for several years, I led a very reserved life during my teenage years. I didn't talk much outside my group of friends, I only gave presentations when they were compulsory, I refused to have my photo taken... until the day I realized that I was actually shooting myself in the foot and missing out on opportunities to share my opinion, influence, leave an imprint on the lives of others and seize professional opportunities.

For the past 10 years, I've been giving conferences on several continents, coaching hundreds of professionals, and often appearing in the media in several countries and on social networks.

No matter how big or small your dream, gradually build up your self-confidence by first speaking up with family and friends, and keep in mind the advantages of communicating to as many people as possible, depending on your situation and circumstances.

Do you want to give yourself that challenge today?

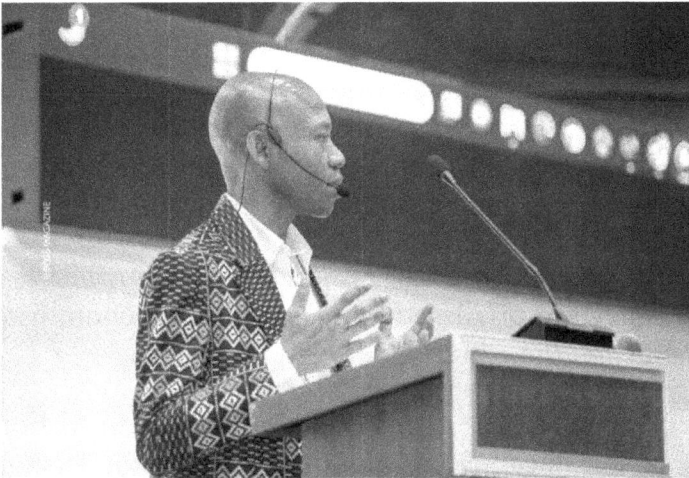

WHY YOU NEED TO DEVELOP THIS SKILL

Without this skill, you won't achieve your medium- and long-term goals. Nothing will save you: neither your diplomas nor your years of experience.

Social competence is important for success in the world of work as well as in business. Becoming socially competent means not only learning to feel at ease in different everyday contexts, but also enjoying yourself in them.

In my role as an international trainer and consultant, I meet people from different socio-professional backgrounds, listen to female presidents talk about their career paths and the challenges facing their organizations, and come into contact with different cultural and economic realities.

Each of these conversations is a source of joy and learning for me. They are privileged moments of connection, listening, leadership and the search for effective solutions.

Social competence opens doors because it opens hearts. It brings people together, breaks down any misunderstandings and sets the parties on the royal road to genuine, mutually beneficial collaborations.

WHY DO I TRAVEL AS A CONSULTANT?

As a consultant in education and international trade, I often travel, both within Canada and from one continent to another.

You too can do it if you apply the following.

Let's not forget that the role of a consultant is to find tailor-made solutions to the specific problems encountered by the companies, organizations or individuals who call on his or her services.

Travelling enables us to meet our customers, to get to know and understand their realities better, to provide training, to create or develop our network, and finally to reinforce our skills and analysis of sometimes complex situations.

The scale and complexity of certain realities can only be truly measured in the field, by meeting the people and populations directly concerned.

As you're no doubt aware, at the heart of consulting work lies an understanding of the customer's needs and concerns. This is followed by analysis and synthesis, in order to make the right diagnosis and propose appropriate solutions. Follow-up on the implementation of these recommendations and final evaluation of the process complete the picture.

In 2024, more than in previous years, I travelled across four continents, often by plane, but also by car and train. I visited both metropolises and villages. And each time, I left with a deep sense of gratitude and accomplishment, given the quality of the relationships forged and the impact of my presence and that of my team.

CHINA: EXCEPTIONAL ENCOUNTERS

O ne of the most fascinating aspects of a consultant's work is the richness and diversity of the professional encounters that ensue.

Not only do you collaborate with organizations of different sizes, cultures and missions, but your leadership also leads you to participate in regional, national and international events of choice.

There's no better way to cross paths with astonishing people, exchange ideas with sharp minds and draw inspiration from enriching stories.

As my stay in China continues, I feel much richer for these welcoming smiles, kind words and openness to others.

Here in Guangzhou, beyond the professional aspect of my presence, there's the social and cultural dimension that already makes my stay unique.

Would you also like to become a consultant and open the doors to an infinite world of possibilities?

NETWORKING: THE MISTAKES YOU'RE PROBABLY MAKING

$$=\!\!=\!\!=\!\!\langle\!\langle\diamond\rangle\!\rangle\!=\!\!=\!\!=$$

Nothing great is built without a network. Repeat after me: "Nothing great is built without a network."

Unfortunately, many professionals and entrepreneurs are still slow to realize this. These people will understand it one day.

As for you, as someone who already values networking, how do you go about it? What events do you attend? How often? How do you prepare? How do you communicate with the people you meet?

Networking means entering other people's professional or business circles, and admitting them into our own.

And in this field, as in many others, quality is better than quantity.

Before taking part in an event, ask yourself the following questions: Who's organizing it? What is its purpose? Who is likely to attend? What is the program? Is it a novelty or a tradition?

It may be useful to contact the event organizers to find out more than the official information.

Once you know the answers to the above questions, get ready. In other words, decide who you want to meet and why. Above all, don't try to talk to everyone. Also ask yourself what value you can offer these people.

I often meet people who are desperate to be seen, to give out their contacts, and so on. Don't do it, or don't do it anymore! You lose your perceived value that way. Instead, concentrate on listening to others, understanding their concerns and offering solutions or the beginnings of solutions. For example, you could recommend that they read a book, visit a website, use a software program, or put them in touch with one of your contacts. The rest will happen naturally: your new acquaintances will want to keep in touch with you and help you out in return (this is how most humans work).

Finally, after the event, send a thank-you and follow-up text or e-mail.

And let time and your exchanges grow these new relationships.

You're sure to reap the rewards of your efforts, patience and generosity.

MY MOST FORMIDABLE WEAPON AS A CONSULTANT

If you have not yet flown Emirates, please do so as soon as possible. The rest of you won't be surprised by what I have to say in the next few lines.

If, in addition, you climb aboard one of our A380-800s, a double-decker behemoth that can accommodate up to 615 passengers, you'll almost regret your previous travels with certain airlines in Africa, Europe and North America.

In short, Emirates is a class act!

Even its economy class exudes comfort. More legroom, larger screens in front of each person, many more and varied channels, wider seats with adjustable leather headrests, more regular and generous service, cleanliness and more.

But make no mistake, this luxury is not Emirates' most formidable weapon, in my opinion.

In fact, the soul of Emirates is its hostesses. Their charm, their smiles, their little attentions are the trademark of the United Arab Emirates airline.

As a consultant, do you know your strengths, your assets, your competitive advantage?

For my part, my interdisciplinary and intercultural approach, combined with my extensive international network, make me a unique consultant, sensitive and respectful of differences, who brings a rich and sometimes unexpected perspective to the issues for which he is responsible.

I take the time to listen, again and again, to ask questions, again and again, which allows me to grasp the nuances behind an image, a hesitation or a change in tone of voice.

As a consultant, you need to pay attention to the subtleties of each situation, the unspoken aspects of speeches, the "forgotten" issues, and so on.

You'll simply become unforgettable.

HOW I DEVELOP MY NETWORK AS A CONSULTANT

───────⟪◇⟫───────

And you can too.

I can't say it often enough: the advantage of working as a consultant is the national and international network you build up over the course of your assignments and events.

Far more valuable than money, these business relationships set you apart from the crowd, enrich your business perspective and ultimately attract unsuspected opportunities.

During the recent Salon International du Bâtiment et de la Construction en Côte d'Ivoire, where I was in charge of communications, I rubbed shoulders with Utku Bengisu, a Turkish businessman. He is president of Bosphorus Expo, then a partner of Ivorian company Archipel Groupe Sarl.

Mr. Bengisu has impressed me with his business intelligence and profound knowledge of Africa. For over 10 years now, he has traveled the continent, visiting 46 countries.

What I learned from meeting Utku Bengisu for almost a week in Abidjan, from his welcome at the airport to the working session at Archipel's offices and dinner at a luxury hotel in the area, I share in the training course I give in collaboration with Eleonore Mejouong, BECOME A CONSULTANT IN 30 DAYS OR LESS.

HOW I STAND OUT AS A CONSULTANT

I love taking photos when I travel and stay outside Canada. One day, I took a photo when I arrived in Dubai from Toronto, aboard an Emirates plane, after a flight of about 11 hours.

The gentleman in the photo with me, a member of the crew, has a French name. When I found out, I stopped speaking English to him. He told me that his family, originally from an Eastern European country, had managed to retain its French-speaking culture over the decades.

His name, his language and his smile made him my new friend. They earned him my appreciation.

What sets you apart as a consultant?

In the almost 10 years I've been training professionals to work as consultants and helping companies optimize their communication strategies on and off social networks, I've generally been praised for my active listening skills, my sense of diversity, equity and inclusion, and the effectiveness of my strategies.

These skills enable me to work in very different cultures and environments, without ever losing sight of the results to be achieved. My approach is results-oriented, while taking the human element into account.

As a consultant, you need to develop a style that builds on your qualities and takes into account the realities of your professional environment. Your interpersonal skills and your know-how will combine to give your services a special cachet.

And success will be at your door.

FIVE STEPS TO STAND OUT ON LINKEDIN

Every week, I meet people on LinkedIn who haven't yet grasped the importance of this platform and the immense opportunity it represents for their career or business.

By October 2023, LinkedIn already had over one billion members in 200 countries and regions. Every second, three people register on the platform. More than 129,000 schools and 58.4 million companies have a LinkedIn page.

Against this backdrop, I'm sure you'll agree that it would be a shame to play miniature on this powerful social network for professionals and business people.

Here are five steps you can take today to stand out from the crowd:

1. Complete your profile, choose a professional profile photo and highlight your banner with a relevant and attractive visual.

2. Publish regularly on topics that interest you or in your area of expertise.

1. Increase the number of connections by sending connection requests to the profiles that speak most to you.

2. Share and comment on publications that could enrich the members of your network.

3. Write recommendations for your business contacts and ask them to do the same for you.

After a few weeks, you'll notice the difference in terms of visits to your profile, number of connections, interesting conversations and invitations to collaborate.

REGISTERED ON LINKEDIN, AND THEN WHAT?

Yesterday, I was coaching a healthcare professional. Her story is similar to that of dozens of other people who ask me for coaching every week.

A woman with around ten years' experience in the field, Marie (first name changed) has been content to log on to LinkedIn for the past three years, almost never interacting with her network, let alone publishing.

She contacted me to help her raise her profile to the level of her goals and explore new professional opportunities.

After a few minutes of coaching, Marie realized that she had unfortunately made the common mistake of consuming content on the platform without almost ever publishing. "I find writing difficult," she told me candidly.

Yes, writing can be difficult when you're not used to it. It takes time and effort to learn how.

However, there is an alternative: find a trained person to take charge of your brand image by animating your page, among other services.

Writing is much easier when you see it as a journey, a discovery of others (readers) and of yourself.

We always write with the image of our ideal reader in mind, asking ourselves two main questions: Who is she (her reality, her concerns, etc.)? How can I reach her (meet her expectations)?

The common trap is to aim for perfection of form rather than relevance of ideas.

What's more, if you write often on LinkedIn, you'll enjoy doing so, you'll assert your leadership, your professional network is sure to expand, and many opportunities will cross your path.

Marie told me she had understood the lesson.

WHAT LINKEDIN BRINGS ME AS A CONSULTANT

If you're not yet on LinkedIn, you're shooting yourself in both feet. If you're passively on it, it's not much better.

With over a billion professionals and more than 58 million companies registered, LinkedIn is the platform par excellence for development, career building and business.

Almost every week, people write to tell me about their professional miseries. As we all know, some workplaces can be devilishly toxic. I know all about it...

How can we escape the slow death we sometimes witness at work? How can we maintain our dignity and make the most of our skills? How can we continue to love life and enjoy it?

For me, the greatest gift of social networks, especially LinkedIn, when used for professional or business purposes, is the incredible freedom they provide.

On LinkedIn, you connect with people you'd never know otherwise. Every day, you learn about all the subjects that interest you. As you interact, mandates or jobs are offered to you. Your agenda fills up with invitations to discuss and collaborate. From now on, the world becomes your playground.

In a word, LinkedIn gives you back your freedom.

You don't care about the supervisor's lies, the screams of the colleague across the hall or the threats of dismissal because you said no to your boss'attempts at seduction.

In short, you have a choice: LinkedIn or "prison".

HOW TO FIND CUSTOMERS ON LINKEDIN

What strategies should you use to find customers or business partners on LinkedIn? Know that while you're looking for them, they're looking for you too.

Your meeting will take place under three conditions.

1. Expand your network on the platform

Of course, it all starts with optimizing your profile and choosing a niche. For more details, read my previous publications on the subject.

2. Publish regularly

At least three times a week, in your niche. Who is your target audience? Who are the people likely to be interested in your products or services? What is their reality? What are their pains or concerns? How can you help them?

Answer these questions by sharing your experiences. You'll bring value to your audience while demonstrating your expertise.

Vary the type of publication, in terms of format and content (photos, videos, personal experiences, testimonials, concrete solutions to a problem, etc.).

3. Socialize with members of your network

This point is often overlooked by many. And yet, in my experience, this is where most of LinkedIn's juice lies.

I've had countless interesting conversations with professionals and entrepreneurs from all over the world. Don't write to anyone to sell your fruit or salad! Write to members of your community to wish them a happy professional anniversary, to congratulate them on a promotion, to thank them for liking or sharing your publication, or to find out more about their career path or projects. You'll be amazed at how they'll open up to you in the course of your exchanges, to the point of requesting your services or making certain suggestions.

In short, enjoy spending time on LinkedIn. Your interactions and results will be all the better for it.

HOW DID YOU ACHIEVE THIS?

This question was put to me by a professional I'm training to BECOME A CONSULTANT IN 30 DAYS OR LESS.He wanted to know how I came to be in charge of communications for both Archipel Group Sarl and the 6th edition of the Salon International du Bâtiment et de la Construction (SIBAT).

Archipel Groupe Sarl is the Ivorian company that for several years has been facilitating exchanges and partnerships between companies in Turkey and those in Ivory Coast and West Africa.

In 2024, SIBAT opened up to other sectors of the economy, including mining, textiles, cosmetics, agriculture and agri-food. A number of officials from Côte d'Ivoire and Turkey, as well as around a hundred Turkish and West African companies, not to mention over two thousand visitors, are scheduled to attend CRRAE-UMOA on September 4 and 5, 2024.

Just one year after I first set foot in Abidjan, how did I manage to find myself at the heart of the organization of one of the most important economic events in Ivory Coast and West Africa?

My answer in a few recommendations:

- Develop solid expertise in your field;

- Spread the word about this expertise;

- Remain honest and patient;

- Expand your network;

- Take a genuine interest in other people, beyond what they can give you;

- Be generous with your time and your listening skills, whenever possible;

- Always look for ways to help others;

- Be willing to step out of your comfort zone to take on new challenges.

Applying these recommendations guarantees you opportunities, some more incredible than others.

STRATEGIES FOR DEVELOPING YOUR NETWORK

Next to time, the most valuable thing a person can offer you is their network. It's time and network that bring opportunities. And it's these opportunities that lead to fulfillment and money.

Developing a professional or business network requires patience, integrity, generosity and commitment. When someone close to you puts you in touch with a member of his or her network, it saves time and engages his or her credibility. This new reference must therefore be used with seriousness and consideration.

In my conferences and coaching sessions, I'm often asked how to develop a professional or business network.

Here are the most important points to follow:

1. **Work on yourself to constantly improve.**

2. **Ask yourself what you can contribute to others, and let your generosity speak for itself.**

3. Participate in events in your sector.

4. Listen a lot, speak little, take an interest in others.

5. Keep track of your meetings, building on common ground.

6. Invite new acquaintances to events or for drinks.

7. Don't force anything, let time do its work.

A few days ago, I was invited by Mel AKPA, founder and managing director of Wit Emploi, to serve as moderator during the first Salon de l'emploi held in Abidjan. It's been a few months since I met Mel, at another Salon, and today we're discussing some important projects.

My participation in the Salon des Métiers opened the doors to Tanguy KONAN, Yannick Gnaman and Abraham KONDE.

HOW I HELPED HER GET STARTED AS A CONSULTANT

Adèle Gunn is a passionate teacher and devoted mother. However, she felt the need to take the BECOME A CONSULTANT IN 30 DAYS course offered by EducNation Consulting Inc. to make a greater impact and continue to grow professionally.

Adèle's other qualities include punctuality, a high level of intercultural sensitivity and an outstanding ability to pass on knowledge. She loves to explain and ask questions, which has led me to work with her even during some of my travels.

I helped Adèle find her positioning, determine her niche and develop her presence on LinkedIn.

The results? Adèle has gained self-confidence, posts regularly on LinkedIn and elsewhere, and is already receiving invitations to collaborate.

My LinkedIn profile bears this beautiful recognition from Adèle:

"I highly recommend Bertrand Ndeffo, an exceptional coach whom I've known for almost two years. His leadership, empathetic listening and caring guidance are remarkable. Always positive and passionate, Bertrand inspires and guides others with genuine expertise and humanity."

HOW I HELPED HIM GET STARTED AS A CONSULTANT

"I s this really for me? Am I up to this new challenge? Have I made the right choice?"

These are the questions I asked myself when I started offering my consulting services in education and communication, almost 10 years ago.

One of the advantages of working with me is that I'm able to understand you because I've experienced the same emotions as you.

One of my roles with Célestin Assamoi was to reassure him of his ability to succeed.

Célestin has studied and worked in education and communication. He continues to read and train in these fields, with a particular focus on leadership development.

But beyond his skills and professional experience, it was Célestin's strong motivation that reassured me. As he had promised, he made a point of meeting me during his vacation in Abidjan, Ivory Coast. He told me all about his academic and professional background and, above all, the reasons why he wanted to take the "BECOME A CONSULTANT IN 30

DAYS OR LESS" course offered by EducNation Consulting Inc.

According to Célestin, my achievements speak for themselves and my perseverance is a source of inspiration for him. He also appreciates the work done by the firm's team, which includes Eleonore Mejouong.

Today, Célestin is more self-confident. His offer of services is precise and attractive. He now publishes regularly on various social networks, including this one. He also knows how to sell his services and negotiate strategic partnerships.

Célestin is well on his way to becoming one of the most sought-after consultants in the French-speaking world!

NATHALIE'S STORY

About three months ago, I received a phone call from Nathalie (first name changed). We've been neighbors for several years.

"Hello, Bertrand!"

"Hello, Nathalie!"

The joy of talking to each other was palpable.

"It's been a while."

"Yes, but..."

"Bertrand, I've been through some very difficult times. I could have been killed!"

"Uh..."

"I spent several weeks in hospital!"

And Nathalie tells me the main facts of her hospitalization.

"You know, Bertrand, I feel ready today. Enough is enough, I can't wait any longer."

"OK. So, tell me everything."

Laughter.

"Do you have any time this week?"

"It depends..."

"I know you're very busy, I see your posts on social networks."

"For you I'll have time, Nathalie."

"Great then! By the way, when did you get back from the Ivory Coast?"

"Let's get back to real business, Nathalie. Well?"

Silence.

"As I told you, I feel totally ready. I regret all this lost time, Bertrand!"

"Look ahead, it will be better for you."

"That's right."

Another silence.

"Bertrand, I want to take your course on "Becoming an International Consultant in 30 days". I'm fed up... I need to finally give myself the means to advance towards my goals."

"I understand. Congratulations on your decision! What about your job?"

"I'm leaving him before the end of the year. Please don't tell anyone."

Nathalie successfully completed the "Become an International Consultant in 30 days or less" training course. She also benefited from a one-month coaching session during which I helped her lay the foundations of her business and generate her first revenues.

Last Friday, I checked in with Nathalie. We talked about our respective families, then she told me:

"Bertrand, I don't know how to thank you. Thanks to your coaching, I now live in an infinite world of possibilities!"

WHY YOU SHOULD BECOME A CONSULTANT

Are you frustrated at work? Do you want to put your experience and skills to good use? Do you want to earn extra income? Does traveling and making a greater impact on society appeal to you?

Then this course is for you!

It's the fruit of twenty years' experience and learning. In addition to receiving the same tools and strategies used by my team and me, we'll open up our professional network to you, both in Canada and internationally.

In this training course, Eleonore Mejouong and I will show you strategies for developing your professional network, promoting your expertise internationally and forging strategic partnerships.

The results? Much greater impact, influence and fulfillment.

Your benefits :

- Certificate of training recognized in Canada

- Customized coaching

- Access to an international network

- 6-month warranty

- Une 30 years of international experience at your service

- Accès direct and continuous access to trainers

- 12h training

- In person, according to invitations and our agenda

- On-line for all others.

- Open to all fields.

GUARANTEE

If you apply my tips and strategies without any positive changes or improvements in your business for 6 months, you receive your entire investment. No questions asked.

Realize your dream of becoming a consultant

https://educnationconsulting.com/fr/consulting-coaching

Writing and publishing your book

Do you want to boost your visibility and credibility? Have you had a book project "on your mind" for some time? Get in touch with us. Our dedicated team can help you write and publish your book within 60 days.

Make an appointment today to talk to us about it, and we'll do the rest:

https://calendly.com/bertrand-21/15min

Book an individual hour of coaching or consultation

https://calendly.com/bertrand-21/60min

OTHER FEATURED TRAINING AND SUPPORT COURSES

Personal Coaching

https://educnationconsulting.com/fr/personal-coaching

Leadership Coaching

https://educnationconsulting.com/fr/leadership-coaching

Business Coaching

https://educnationconsulting.com/fr/business-coaching

Scholarship Coaching

https://educnationconsulting.com/fr/scholarship-coaching

Emotional intelligence. A world of possibilities

https://educnationconsulting.com/fr/cours

Successful immigration

https://educnationconsulting.com/fr/cours

TRAINING AND SUPPORT

I dentity and access management in the enterprise

IT security

Quality Safety Environment (QSE)

Project management

Business analysis

How to use artificial intelligence to grow your business

Become a consultant in 30 days or less

Become a certified mentor

Become a certified coach

Entrepreneurship for young people aged 12 to 20

Thinking, creating and growing your business today

The keys to emotional intelligence at work and elsewhere

How to communicate effectively at work

How to communicate effectively in everyday life

Parents, how to communicate effectively with your children

Negotiation: how to win every time

Time and priority management

Online business strategies that really work

How to do business with China (with a list of niche suppliers)

Training and support for business start-ups and business development with Canada

Training and support for company start-ups and business development with China

Training and support for company start-ups and business development with Côte d'Ivoire

Secrets to unlocking your full potential

From failure to success: how to transform yourself and defy the odds

The keys to transformational leadership and how to put them into practice

How to motivate your employees to success

Equity, diversity and inclusion in the workplace

The art of turning differences into a powerful engine for growth

Personal branding: secrets and impact

How to communicate effectively on social networks

The essential tools of corporate communication

Human rights and education: risks and opportunities

Digital citizenship and organizations today

How to recognize and combat human trafficking

Training packages can be tailored to your specific needs (individuals and organizations).

WHY TRUST OUR TEAM?

In its 9 years of existence and activity, EducNation Consulting Inc. has become a world leader in education, training and coaching. Today, it serves young people, professionals and organizations in some twenty countries on four continents.

Our team is multicultural, multidisciplinary and both people- and results-oriented. A visit to our website https://www.educnationconsulting.com/fr/temoignages and our social networks will convince you of the value we can bring to your project or organization.

Please contact us today with any questions, suggestions or concerns:

bertrand@educnationconsulting.com

eleonore@educnationconsulting.com

OUR LINKS

Website

www.educnationconsulting.com

Facebook

https://www.facebook.com/CoachingEducationCanadaWorldwide?mibextid=JRoKGi

LinkedIn

https://www.linkedin.com/in/bertrandndeffo/

https://www.linkedin.com/in/eleonore-m-90b652236

EducNation Consulting Inc. Newspaper

https://www.linkedin.com/newsletters/linkedin-le-verbe-en-action-7261891890621407233/

Instagram

https://www.instagram.com/educnation/

Tiktok

https://www.tiktok.com/@educnationconsulting.com?_t=8rD2kqOGkMh&_r=1

Let's have a tea or a coffee

https://calendly.com/bertrand-21/15min

APPENDIX

Premium Agency

www.agencepremium-ci.com

B&E Harmony Inc.

www.benorharmony.com

CEPICI (Ivory Coast Investment Promotion Center)

www.cepici.gouv.ci

Certified Coaches Federation

www.certifiedcoachesfederation.com

Canadian Chamber of Commerce

www.chamber.ca

Ivory Coast Chamber of Commerce and Industry

www.cci.ci

EducNation Consulting Inc.

www.educnationconsulting.com

Ontario College of Teachers

www.oct.ca

Ovation Consult

www.ovationconsult.com

International Trade Fair for Suppliers and Investors from Africa

www.sifia.net

Union des Commerçants de Côte d'Ivoire

https://www.facebook.com/share/14F1DcWjPY/

US Institute of Diplomacy and Human Rights

www.usidhr.org

Wit Emploi

https://www.linkedin.com/company/wit-emploi/posts/?feedView=all

INDEX